T0011115

VIRGINIA HALL

Clever Spy of WORLD WAR II

by Rebecca Langston-George   illustrated by Luiz Fernando De Silva

CAPSTONE PRESS
a capstone imprint

Published by Capstone Press, an imprint of Capstone
1710 Roe Crest Drive, North Mankato, Minnesota 56003
capstonepub.com

Copyright © 2023 by Capstone. All rights reserved. No part of this publication may be
reproduced in whole or in part, or stored in a retrieval system, or transmitted in any form
or by any means, electronic, mechanical, photocopying, recording, or otherwise, without
written permission of the publisher.

Library of Congress Cataloging-in-Publication Data
Names: Langston-George, Rebecca, author. | Chow, Samantha Feriolla, illustrator.
Title: Virginia Hall : clever spy of World War II / by Rebecca Langston-George ; illustrated by
Samantha Feriolla Chow. Other titles: Clever spy of World War II
Description: North Mankato, Minnesota : Capstone Press, an imprint of Capstone, [2023]
| Series: Women warriors of World War II | Includes bibliographical references. | Audience:
Ages 8-11 | Audience: Grades 4-6 |
Summary: "An action-packed graphic novel about Virginia Hall, known as one of the most
courageous spies of World War II. In the early 1940s, during World War II, Germany's Nazi
regime expanded into neighboring European countries, committing horrific crimes against
Jewish people and other groups. Enter: Virginia Hall. Born on a small Maryland farm, this
brilliant woman's worldly ambitions led her to a clerical position at the U.S. embassy in
Warsaw, Poland. While there, a hunting accident caused Hall to lose her leg. After being
fitted with a wooden prosthetic leg, she persevered in her work. Hall soon became a spy
for Allied forces, serving behind enemy lines in France. With cleverness and courage, Hall,
who the Nazis nicknamed the "Limping Lady," eventually became one of the Allies' greatest
assets and one the German Gestapo's most feared spies. In this action-packed, full-color
graphic novel, learn more about this daring woman who took risks, defied expectations, and
confronted the enemies of World War II"-- Provided by publisher.
Identifiers: LCCN 2023002023 (print) | LCCN 2023002024 (ebook) |
ISBN 9781669013709 (hardcover) | ISBN 9781669013655 (paperback) | ISBN
9781669013662 (ebook pdf) | ISBN 9781669013686 (kindle edition) | ISBN
9781669013693 (epub)
Subjects: LCSH: Goillot, Virginia, 1906-1982--Comic books, strips, etc.--Juvenile literature.
| Women spies--United States--Biography--Comic books, strips, etc.--Juvenile literature.
| Spies--United States--Biography--Comic books, strips, etc.--Juvenile literature. | World
War, 1939-1945--Secret service--United States--Comic books, strips, etc.--Juvenile
literature. | World War, 1939-1945--Secret service--Great Britain--Comic books, strips,
etc.--Juvenile literature. | World War, 1939-1945--Underground movements--France--
Comic books, strips, etc.--Juvenile literature. | Espionage, American--Europe--History--20th
century--Comic books, strips, etc.--Juvenile literature.
Classification: LCC D810.S8 G595 2023 (print) | LCC D810.S8 (ebook) |
DDC 940.54/8641092 [B]--dc23/eng/20230118
LC record available at https://lccn.loc.gov/2023002023
LC ebook record available at https://lccn.loc.gov/2023002024Editorial

Credits
Editor: Donald Lemke; Designer: Sarah Bennett;
Production Specialist: Katy LaVigne

Design Elements: Shutterstock/Here

Cover Artist:
Samantha F. Chow

All internet sites appearing in back matter were available and accurate
when this book was sent to press.

Printed and bound in the USA. 5425

TABLE OF CONTENTS

PROLOGUE: AN ADVENTUROUS GIRL

In April 1906, Virginia Hall was born into a wealthy banking family.

By the age of three, she was a world traveler. Her family often sailed across the Atlantic Ocean, from Baltimore to Europe, for vacation.

Virginia's travels made her a spirited girl. She had a flare for drama and acted in many school plays.

Argh, matey!

She rode horses and cared for animals at the family's second home, Box Horn Farm.

Keep up, girls!

Athletic and independent, Virginia enjoyed shooting and skiing. Unlike most young women then, she preferred wearing pants rather than dresses.

Mrs. Hall was disappointed when her beautiful, charming daughter chose college instead of marriage.

But Mr. Hall paid for his beloved "Dindy" to study French at the Sorbonne Université in Paris, France, and then German in Vienna, Austria.

The only way to get ahead in this world is to get an education.

A WOMAN WITH DREAMS

In 1926, Virginia arrived in France. She had dreams of working for the American State Department as a diplomat or ambassador.

Oh, my!

During the next few years, Virginia mastered five languages besides English. She learned to speak French, German, Spanish, Italian, and Russian.

Soon, Virginia applied to work at the U.S. State Department. However, despite her language skills, her application was denied.

DENIED

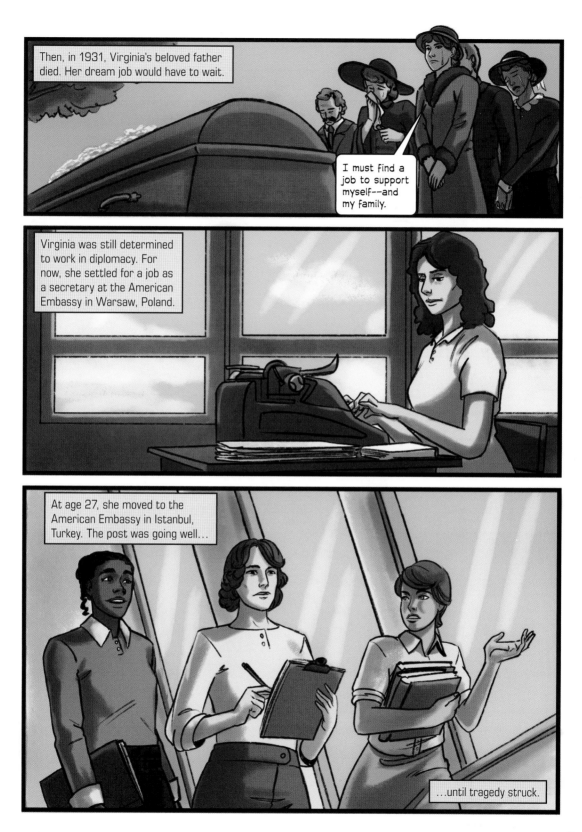

Then, in 1931, Virginia's beloved father died. Her dream job would have to wait.

I must find a job to support myself--and my family.

Virginia was still determined to work in diplomacy. For now, she settled for a job as a secretary at the American Embassy in Warsaw, Poland.

At age 27, she moved to the American Embassy in Istanbul, Turkey. The post was going well...

...until tragedy struck.

An avid hunter, Virginia organized a bird hunt for embassy staff on December 8, 1933.

But that day, she tripped, and her gun went off. Virginia shot her left foot and was rushed to the hospital.

During the next couple weeks, the wound became badly infected.

Fearing she might die, doctors removed her left leg below the knee on Christmas Day.

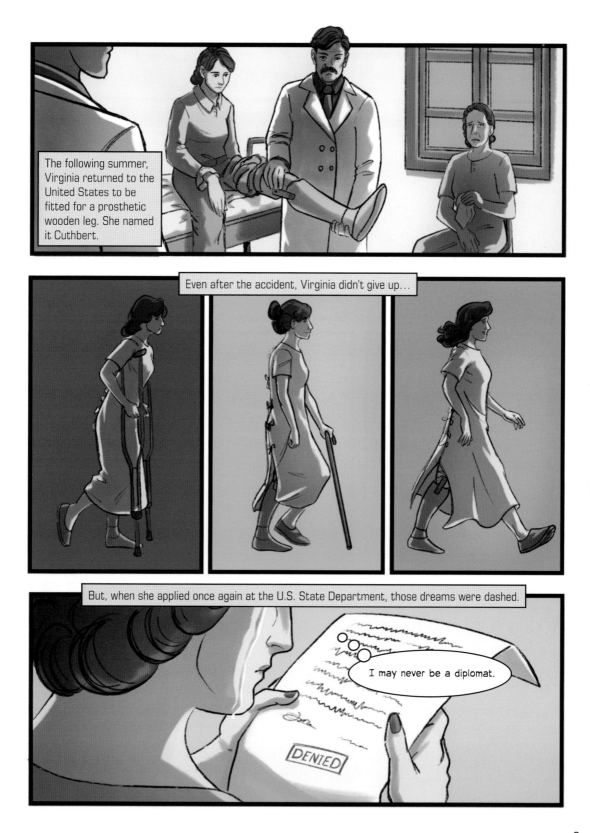

The following summer, Virginia returned to the United States to be fitted for a prosthetic wooden leg. She named it Cuthbert.

Even after the accident, Virginia didn't give up...

But, when she applied once again at the U.S. State Department, those dreams were dashed.

I may never be a diplomat.

DENIED

FEARLESS VOLUNTEER

Still, Virginia was determined to work overseas. Even if it wasn't her dream job.

Hello! I'm your new secretary.

Throughout the 1930s, Virginia worked at U.S. embassies in Italy and Estonia. During that time, Europeans grew worried about the German leader Adolf Hitler.

The paper says Hitler is moving troops.

Oh, my!

The German dictator claimed Austria, Sudetenland, and nearby areas belonged to Germany since the people there spoke the German language.

On September 1, 1939, Germany, greedy for more land, invaded Poland.

As a result, Britain and France declared war on Germany.

When Virginia heard about the fighting in her beloved France, she had to act! She traveled there and volunteered to drive an ambulance.

KA-BOOM!

Starting in May 1940, she drove wounded soldiers to hospitals in Paris, France.

She wrote letters to her mother back home in the United States.

She is trying to make things sound better for me.

To avoid more deaths, France agreed to an armistice with Germany on June 22, 1940. The fighting temporarily stopped.

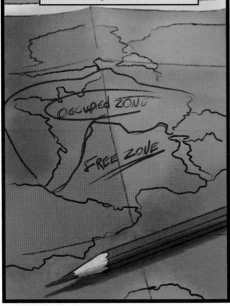

France was divided into two sections. Germany occupied the north. The French continued to hold the south.

Volunteer drivers, like Virginia, were no longer needed.

Virginia quickly decided to go to Britain. Traveling through Spain, she met George Bellows, a British spy posing as a salesman.

Could I sit, ma'am

Please do.

Upon learning of her bravery, Bellows suggested she call his friends about a job. He didn't mention the work he had in mind was in espionage.

I'm sending you a most unusual woman. I think we can use her!

In London, she took a job at the U.S. Embassy. But the phone numbers George Bellows gave her were temporarily forgotten when Hitler's Nazis began bombing the city.

WEE-OO! WEE-OO!

Air raid sirens punctuated the evenings at her boarding house. She and the other lodgers scrambled to the cellar night after night.

WEE-OO! WEE-OO!

UNDERCOVER JOURNALIST

Before long, Virginia called one of Bellows' friends, Vera Atkins. Miss Atkins invited Virginia to parties and lunches to observe her.

Britain's spy network, the Special Operation Executive, or SOE, investigated Virginia. They watched her from afar.

This lady might well be used for a mission.

They decided the American with nerves of steel could do more for the war effort than typing.

On February 17, 1941, the British SOE asked Virginia to spy for them.

Since Americans aren't involved in the war, you'll be able to travel to France without suspicion.

I'd be honored to help.

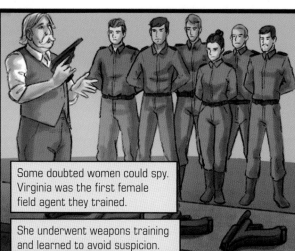

Some doubted women could spy. Virginia was the first female field agent they trained.

She underwent weapons training and learned to avoid suspicion.

She learned to pick locks, decode wireless messages, and even survive harsh interrogation techniques.

She was given a rubber-coated poison pill and the authority to kill if needed.

Only use this if absolutely necessary.

Virginia now had two names. Her code name was Germaine. Her new cover was an American journalist with the *New York Post*.

In August 1941, she arrived in German-occupied France. Under her dress she wore two money belts hiding one million counterfeit francs.

Virginia eavesdropped around soldiers who didn't realize she understood German. Listening to the locals, she discovered who to persuade to join the resistance. She gathered French patriots ready to rebel against the Germans.

She varied her look with hats, gloves, and glasses. With makeup, hairstyles, and hair dye she had many disguises. She penciled in wrinkles and plumped her cheeks with rubber mouth pads.

The trick is to fade into the background and not draw attention to myself.

Virginia Hall could play any part.

Virginia was part of a network of spies. She traveled on foot, bicycle, and train to bring them information, forged documents, and counterfeit cash.

She arranged to house and transport new spies. She had hairdressers disguise them with new cuts.

The work was dangerous. Those caught were tortured, jailed, or murdered.

Virginia had to constantly move to avoid suspicion.

The wolves are at the door.

PRISON BREAK MASTERMIND

Every meeting was risky. German soldiers learned to track wireless signals, putting operators and those who helped them in danger.

One spy parachuted off course and was arrested. The Germans found a scrap of paper in his pocket with the address of Cristophe Villa des Bois, the wireless operator he was to contact.

The Germans captured Cristophe. One of them posed as him, sending coded radio messages directing other spies to come pick up money and supplies.

Virginia ignored the invitation.

Seems suspicious.

Those who went were imprisoned.

Soon, nearly every radio operator in France was in prison. But Virginia planned to rescue the men she called the Corsicans.

First, she helped the wife of one of the Corsicans befriend a guard. Then she provided money to bribe him. As a result, the guard moved the spies to a less secure prison.

Prisoners could receive clothing, cans of food, and books. Virginia bribed the guard to look the other way when they smuggled in wire cutters, tin snippers, and files.

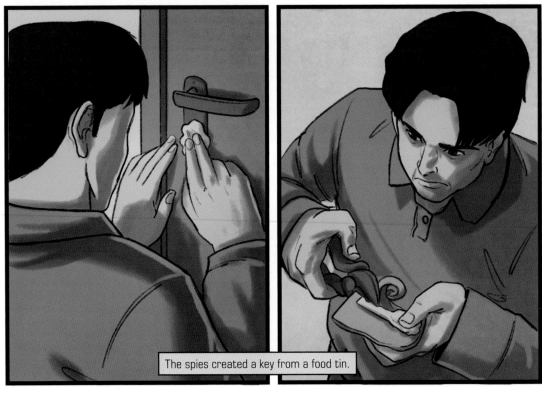

The spies created a key from a food tin.

They cut the wire fence.

Finally, the Corsicans escaped to safehouses Virginia set up.

Many of Our Men Owe Their Lives to Virginia

WANTED

After the prison break, Virginia's wanted poster was plastered everywhere.

DARING OLD CHEESE PEDDLER

When America entered the war, Virginia's cover as an American journalist was no longer safe.

PEARL HARBOR BOMBED YESTERDAY! AMERICA ENTERS THE WAR.

Virginia was ordered back to Britain.

Virginia caught the late train south to the border between France and Spain.

Virginia paid a smuggler to guide her and two strangers, also awaiting escape, over the icy Pyrenees mountains trail on foot.

Despite snow up to her knee and treacherous trails, Virginia never complained. Her leg above the prosthetic blistered and bled.

Cuthbert is causing difficulties!

She and her fellow travelers made it over the mountains and waited at the train station for it to open.

But the police arrested them for not having Spanish entry stamps on their passports.

In jail for 20 days, Virginia finally got word to the U.S. Embassy that she needed help.

While in jail, the British government secretly awarded her the MBE, or Most Excellent Order of the British Empire, for saving her fellow spies.

Back in England, she told the SOE everything she could remember.

She begged them to send her back, but they refused. Virginia, however, didn't give up easily.

It's time I learn how to properly send messages!

Virginia had long wanted more training on receiving and sending radio signals. She insisted they fully train her to use the wireless.

If Britain wouldn't send her back to France, maybe her native country would. She showed up at the Office of Strategic Services and volunteered to spy for them.

I can't believe our luck! A fully trained spy who was a wireless operator!

The Americans couldn't sign her fast enough. For once, America wasn't interested in using her as a secretary!

In March 1944, the Americans dropped "Diane" off the coast of France along with another spy. Virginia put her schoolgirl drama skills to good use acting like an old peasant wife.

A farmer traded her room and board to care for his mother and animals. No stranger to farm life, she milked the cows and goats, then scouted good locations for parachute drops when she took the animals out to pasture.

She made cheese to sell to the Germans. This allowed her to listen in on their plans, which she wired to the OSS. No one suspected the most wanted spy in France was right under their noses.

The Gestapo tracked a radio signal to her home one day. With the radio already hidden, all they found was cheese. But the old cheese peddler knew her luck was running out.

It's just the old cheese woman.

Time to go.

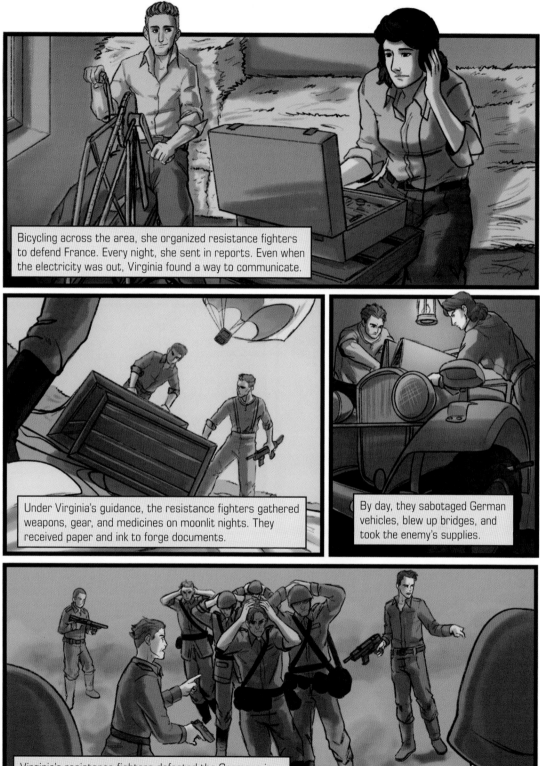

Bicycling across the area, she organized resistance fighters to defend France. Every night, she sent in reports. Even when the electricity was out, Virginia found a way to communicate.

Under Virginia's guidance, the resistance fighters gathered weapons, gear, and medicines on moonlit nights. They received paper and ink to forge documents.

By day, they sabotaged German vehicles, blew up bridges, and took the enemy's supplies.

Virginia's resistance fighters defeated the Germans in their area two days before Allied troops arrived in Paris.

HONORED AT LAST

In September 1945, with the war over, Virginia returned home. The OSS was renamed the Central Intelligence Agency (CIA). Virginia was one of the first women to work for them.

Many of my friends were killed for talking too much.

President Truman offered to pin a medal on Virginia himself, but she didn't want the attention, since she hoped to keep working as a spy.

Virginia received the Distinguished Service Cross on September 27, 1945, in a small ceremony with her mother and her boss present.

Though Virginia longed to spy again, the CIA never again used her to her full potential. After two years as a consultant in Europe, Virginia was sent back to a desk and a typewriter.

In April 1950, she married Paul Goillot, a fellow spy who served with her at the end of the war.

Though Virginia didn't get the recognition she deserved in her lifetime, in December 2016 the CIA named a building in her honor.

New agents train there today.

Virginia Hall

GLOSSARY

Allies (al-LIES)—group of countries that work together to fight against a common enemy

armistice (AR-mis-tis)—temporary agreement to stop fighting in a war

counterfeit (KOWN-tur-fit)—something that looks like the real thing but is actually fake

diplomat (DIP-luh-mat)—a person who works for their government to make agreements with other countries, like a mediator in a group project

disguises (dis-GUY-ziz)—clothes or accessories that someone wears to look like someone else

eavesdrop (EEVZ-drop)—listen secretly to a conversation that you're not supposed to hear

espionage (EH-spee-uh-nahj)—spying on another country to get secret information, like being a detective to find out a mystery

interrogation (in-ter-uh-GEY-shun)—asking someone a lot of questions to find out the truth, like in a police investigation

resistance fighters (ri-ZIS-tuhns FIGHT-ers)—people who fight against an enemy who has taken over their country

READ MORE

Kallen, Stuart A. *World War II Spies and Secret Agents.* Minneapolis: Lerner, 2018.

Mitchell, Don. *The Lady Is a Spy: Virginia Hall, World War II Hero of the French Resistance.* New York: Scholastic, 2019.

Roman, Carole P. *Spies, Code Breakers, and Secret Agents: A World War II Book for Kids.* Emeryville, CA: Rockridge Press, 2020.

INTERNET SITES

Central Intelligence Agency: Virginia Hall: The Courage and Daring of "The Limping Lady"
cia.gov/stories/story/virginia-hall-the-courage-and-daring-of-the-limping-lady

NPR: 'A Woman Of No Importance' Finally Gets Her Due
npr.org/2019/04/18/711356336/a-woman-of-no-importance-finally-gets-her-due

Smithsonian Magazine: WANTED: The Limping Lady
smithsonianmag.com/history/wanted-the-limping-lady-146541513

ABOUT THE AUTHOR

Rebecca Langston-George is the author of thirteen books with Capstone Press. A retired teacher, she is the regional advisor for the central-coastal chapter of the Society of Children's Book Writers and Illustrators.

ABOUT THE ILLUSTRATOR

Luiz Fernando De Silva is an illustrator and comic artist from Santa Catarina, Brazil. Since he was a child, he has enjoyed creating his own stories—many based on his favortie cartoons, video games, and science fiction films. Luiz started his career as a professional illustrator and designer in 2006. He has been a full-time illustrator for 10 years now. In his free time, he likes to watch movies and series, play video games, read, and barbecue.